Fleeing Mad Dog McGee

By Jill McDougall

Illustrated by Rosie Colligan

Pearson Australia
(a division of Pearson Australia Group Pty Ltd)
707 Collins Street, Melbourne, Victoria 3008
PO Box 23360, Melbourne, Victoria 8012
www.pearson.com.au

First published 2012 by Pearson Australia
2019 2018 2017 2016
10 9 8 7 6 5 4 3 2

Commissioning Editor: Sabine Bolick
Project Editor: Suzy Freeman
Editor: Cameron Macintosh
Designer: Anne Donald
Copyright & Pictures Editor: Marg Barber
Cover art: Rosie Colligan
Illustrator: Rosie Colligan
Printed in Australia by the SOS Print + Media Group

ISBN 978 1 4425 3780 4

Pearson Australia Group Pty Ltd ABN 40 004 245 943

CONTENTS

CHAPTER 1

Liverpool, England, August 1851

"**Well, well,** what have we got 'ere?"

Will spun around. Mad Dog McGee's red face bore down on him. The shark-grey eyes were cold.

"Turn out your pockets, Will Hawker," Mad Dog snarled.

Will's hands shook. The chestnuts he was holding skittered across the wooden wharf and into the Mersey River below. Will couldn't worry about them now. Mad Dog was not only a thief, he was a brute. Everyone knew he had killed a man in an alehouse brawl.

"Move your bones or you'll be eating Mersey mud." Mad Dog's breath stank of sour onions.

Mad Dog growled and reached out a large tattooed hand. “Give me your moneybag, Hawker.”

Will’s eyes scanned the wharf, although it didn’t seem likely that anyone would come to his aid.

A sailing ship was moored at the slip, waiting for the tide to come in. Passengers dressed in their finest made their way up the gangway. Others busied themselves on the wharf with boxes and trunks.

Their faces shone with excitement. The *Lady Mary* would soon carry them far across the globe on a great adventure. They would have no time to spare for a scruffy twelve-year-old boy.

Will felt the muscles in his arm twitch but he said quietly, “You want my moneybag, Mr McGee? You get it.”

With one smooth action, he pulled the bag out of his pocket and sent it hurtling across the river mudflats.

Mad Dog’s eyes burned with hate. “You’ll pay for this, Will Hawker.”

Mad Dog heaved his massive body over the edge of the wharf and his boots squelched through the mud.

For the first time, Will noticed that Mad Dog was decked out in a shiny new suit. “It won’t be shiny for long,” Will thought with a grin. He knew he should make himself scarce but he couldn’t resist lingering a moment.

Mad Dog emerged from the mudflats grasping the moneybag in a grubby fist.

As his fingers fumbled with the coarse string, Will’s thoughts flew to his mother and sisters anxiously awaiting his earnings. Will’s father had been killed in a dockside accident and Will’s earnings from selling chestnuts to ships’ passengers helped put food on the table.

Mad Dog howled with success as his thick fingers dipped into the moneybag. Suddenly his expression changed from glee to horror as he drew out the contents…

Pebbles.

Will made a run for it and patted the bump half way down his jacket. His money was safe where Mama had sewn a secret pocket. Allowing a smile to slide across his face, he turned sharply, slowed down and joined the crowd. He was sure that Mad Dog would slink away to lick his wounds.

He was wrong.

CHAPTER 2

The *Lady Mary*

It was the foul language Will heard first. He swung around to see Mad Dog shoving aside a woman with a baby. Mad Dog's trousers were smeared with slime. A cloud of flies floated about his hat.

Will ducked behind a pile of luggage and waited for the lumbering footsteps to pass. Mad Dog was not known for his quick-wittedness.

"Owww!" Something jabbed Will in the ribs.

An elegant woman with a sharp umbrella stood over him. "What are you doing here?" she asked, prodding him more gently this time. With her spare hand, she gripped a pale-faced girl wearing a blue bonnet.

"Er… playing hide-and-go-seek," said Will, thinking quickly.

To Will's surprise, the woman produced a penny from her purse and held it out to him. "Since you've time to waste on games, you can help me with my cabin trunks," she said, casting an eye towards the *Lady Mary*. "We sail on the tide and the porters are busy."

"At your service, Ma'am." Will gleefully picked up the trunks and hefted them towards the gangway. The woman led the way, still holding the hand of the little girl who constantly turned to check Will's progress.

"Mind your step," called the woman, lifting her long skirts clear of the deck.

The great ship heaved on the swell and Will felt his stomach lurch. He followed the woman towards the back of the ship.

They passed a fancy dining saloon and stopped at the open door of a vast airy cabin. A sign in gold letters said:

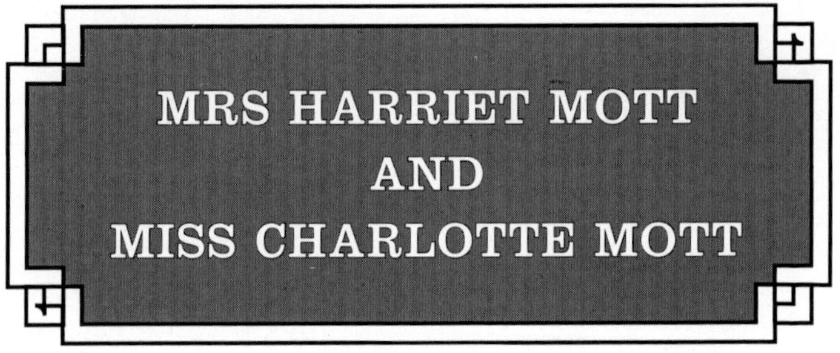

Will carefully placed the trunks on the polished oak floors and glanced around. The cabin was like a palace. The walls were pure white with massive ornamental mirrors. On the back wall—the stern of the ship—was a plush red sofa with gold piping. Will half-expected to find it occupied by Queen Victoria herself.

"You can leave the trunks over there," said the woman, who Will assumed must be Mrs Mott.

Will picked up the trunks and placed them where requested, careful not to touch anything.

Will felt a small hand tug his jacket. He looked down to see Charlotte's pale, pointed face regarding him seriously.

"Will you come to meet Gertie?" she asked. "She's up on the top deck."

Mrs Mott caught Will's confused look. "Gertie is a pet," she explained. "Charlotte refused to leave Liverpool without her."

Will smiled kindly at Charlotte. "I must be getting back before the ship sails," he said, tipping his cap. "I wish you, your mother and… Gertie a very pleasant voyage."

On the main deck, the air was thick with the stench of burning coal from the steam-powered tugboats. Will peered over the ship's rail, his eyes scanning the crowd for Mad Dog. With any luck the brute would have long gone and Will could—

Speak of the devil! There was the villain himself climbing the gangway. He was carrying a battered case and waving a ticket at the stewards as if he were the lord of the high seas. Will felt a jolt of astonishment.

Could it be true? Mad Dog McGee was a passenger on the *Lady Mary*!

McGee looked up, and his eyes met Will's. A slow, nasty smile spread across Mad Dog's face. "Will Hawker!" shouted Mad Dog. "I want a word with you!"

Will turned and hurried away. He could feel Mad Dog's eyes like daggers, stabbing into his back. He skirted a bunch of sailors lowering barrels into the ship's hold and a group of emigrants dancing to a fiddler's tune. Will glanced around to see one of the emigrants grab Mad Dog by the hand and drag him into the dance.

Desperate not to be seen, Will slipped into an open hatch that led below the deck and scrambled down the step-ladder. Through a hatch in the floor was another ladder that led deep into the ship.

The air stank of mould. Will opened a small locker. It was packed with folded canvas and coils of heavy rope. He slipped inside and snapped the door shut.

Will strained his ears for the sound of footsteps but only his breathing seeped through the silence.

The ship rocked gently back and forth. Timbers creaked and groaned. Will suddenly felt drowsy and his eyelids began to sag.

The next thing Will knew, he was pitched violently sideways. For a terrible moment, he thought the ship was moving. Then he realised, it *was* moving. He sprang for the locker door, then sank back. It was too late. He could sense that the great ship was heading towards the open sea.

CHAPTER 3

The Stowaway

"We deal harshly with stowaways." The captain's eyes were fierce. He paced up and down the deck, then paused again in front of Will. "Lucky for you, we need an extra pair of hands. You'll work your passage to Port Phillip and if you slacken off, you'll be transported in chains like a convict."

Will nodded, squinting in the bright sunlight. He was glad to be out of the locker—his one night there had felt more like a week. When a sailor looking for spare rope discovered his hiding place, he'd felt relieved. But at the same time he was sick with worry about his mother and sisters who depended on him, and whom he had left behind.

"Take him to steerage," ordered the captain. "The constable is expecting him."

A ruddy-faced seaman led Will to a low-ceilinged room far below decks. Rows of wooden bunks were fixed on either side. Most were occupied. The stench of vomit hung in the air, and Will's stomach started to turn.

The seaman gave a gap-toothed grin. "Everyone gets seasick at first," he said, as if it was some sort of joke. He gestured to a thin straw mattress on an upper bunk. "That's your bit o' heaven right there."

Will nodded. Through the gloom, he made out the bulky shape of a man hunched over the rough-hewn table that ran down the centre of the room. The man's fingers were dipping greedily into something that smelled like boiled mutton.

"That fellow's just been made one of the ship's constables for the voyage," said the seaman. "He's in charge of you. Do your jobs proper and you'll be spared the chains."

The constable turned to face Will, but at that moment the ship gave a heave. Will was sent crashing towards the table. He tried to right himself, but his fist landed in the bowl of mutton. The bowl flipped sideways, drowning the constable in grease and gravy.

“You fool!” shouted the constable, leaping to his feet.

He hauled Will up by his jacket and shook him hard and long.

There was a shocked silence as the two stared at one another. A sick feeling crept up Will’s throat as he looked into the cold grey eyes of Mad Dog McGee.

CHAPTER 4

Gertie

Will shivered in the bitter wind. His clothes were drenched from the waves that lashed the deck. The past month on the *Lady Mary* had been like a nightmare with no end. The only bright moment had occurred when a ship returning to England came alongside and Will was able to pass a roughly written note to his mother, wrapped around some coins:

It was those very coins that now made Will's life so wretched. Mad Dog had not forgiven him for his trickery and took every opportunity to take his revenge. Once, when Will was scrubbing the steerage floor, Mad Dog lashed out with his foot, missing Will's face by inches. Another time, Will was carrying water to the first-class cabins when Mad Dog tripped him up, sending him sprawling across the deck.

Bruised and exhausted, Will struggled on with his chores. His favourite time was when he could leave the stuffy bunkroom for the fresh air on deck. Today the sky was a deep thundery grey and the huge canvas sails bellied out in the rising wind. Will climbed from the main deck to the foredeck where some of the animals were penned. It was his job to feed them and clean up their mess.

The sheep greeted him mournfully, their hooves slipping on the rolling deck. Will felt sorry for them, but he knew they wouldn't suffer for long. They would provide the first-class passengers with fresh meat for their Sunday roast, while in steerage they were lucky to be fed a watery soup boiled from the leftover bones.

Nearby, in a coop protected by a strip of canvas, lived Gertie, Charlotte's beloved pet. Will had been surprised to discover that Gertie was no more than a small red hen. Charlotte doted on the bird and could often be found squatting by the coop feeding Gertie tidbits.

"Mind nothing happens to that bird," Mad Dog had warned in a sneering tone. "Or your life won't be worth living."

Will knew that Mad Dog meant every word.

With the wind tearing at his eyes, Will wondered how much more miserable his life could become. Mad Dog made sure he didn't get any of the rations doled out to steerage passengers. He was forced to feed on scraps, and there were precious few of those. Even Gertie ate better. Will measured out a cup of grain from a barrel and calling softly, lifted the flap covering the coop. Then his heart froze. The coop was empty. Will blinked and looked again in case his eyes were playing tricks.

He had taken care to fasten the cage that morning, but now the door gaped open. With trembling fingers, he examined the rope he had used to secure it. There was no doubt—it had been cut with a knife.

Will groaned. Mad Dog was up to his usual tricks. When the captain learned that Will had let a much-loved chicken get away ... But that didn't bear thinking about.

Will fastened his dirty coat over his thin chest, and gazed about. Black clouds boiled overhead and the ship was beginning to buck on the grey heaving seas.

Below, on the main deck, steerage passengers hastily closed the boxes brought up from the hold. It was Luggage Day and they were swapping soiled clothes for fresh ones.

A tiny figure with a long braid of hair weaved through the rabble of passengers. It was Charlotte. Her course was unsteady but it was clear she was coming his way.

Will hurried down the stairs to meet her.

"Charlotte," he said, anxiously, "you must go back to Mama. A storm is coming."

The little girl regarded him with wide anxious eyes. "How is Gertie?"

Will knelt in front of her, his mind racing. "Gertie is ... well, she's ..."

Charlotte pushed past him. "I must bring her into the cabin."

"Wait!" Will reached out for her but his boot caught in a coil of rope and he fell down hard against the deck.

"All passengers below!" called the first mate. "Batten the hatches."

"Charlotte, come here!" yelled Will, but the roar of the storm carried his voice away.

There was a flurry of movement as passengers scuttled through the hatchway and sailors scrambled to reel in the sails.

The first mate spotted Will, but didn't see Charlotte. "Get below!" he ordered.

Will wondered if he should explain, but there was no time.

Little Charlotte, intent on her mission, was now climbing the stairs to the foredeck. Her skirts, whipping about her legs, made it look like she'd be carried off by the gale.

"Charlotte! Stay there!" Will's cry was again lost to the howl of the wind. The ship rolled wildly and a stream of seawater washed across the deck.

Charlotte shrieked and stumbled, losing her grip on the rail. At that moment the ship dipped into a giant trough and a monster wave appeared, its whitecaps whipped off by the wind. Will watched fearfully. Charlotte would surely be washed overboard.

He instinctively launched his body across the space and grabbed Charlotte, just as the torrent of freezing water crashed down on them. He held her small body close with all the strength he could muster. Their bodies were dragged across the deck, and it seemed as if they would both be poured into the ocean.

Charlotte swallowed seawater and gagged. The salt water stung Will's eyes, but a rope slid by his face. With one hand, he made a frantic grab at it, but missed.

Suddenly the whole world tilted the other way. Will felt Charlotte being dragged from his grasp. Spluttering salt water, he again tried to grab onto her with everything he had.

Will and Charlotte were dashed hard against the ship's cannon and Will felt a knife of pain jab through him. He heard the piercing scream of the young girl, and felt a tremendous pressure in his lungs. The wind carried away his cries for help. Then everything started to drift away…

CHAPTER 5

First Class

Will was lying on something soft and comfortable. The scent of linseed oil and lavender soap filled his nostrils.

He forced his eyelids open and looked about groggily. He caught a glimpse of white wall and varnished woodwork. Harriet Mott bent over him, her face gentle.

"So, you're finally awake," she said.

Will tried to speak but could only let out a rattly cough. Every bit of him ached.

"Drink this." A cup was raised to his lips. The liquid tore at his throat.

"How is Charlotte?" rasped Will.

Mrs Mott took a deep shuddery breath and her eyes grew moist. "She is recovering in the ship's hospital. I've just left her to check on you."

"And Gertie …?" He felt foolish asking, but he had to know.

Mrs Mott gave a small smile. "Gertie was discovered in the saloon eating breadcrumbs. It's lucky she didn't end up on the stove."

Will felt a surge of relief, and soon drifted back to sleep.

When he'd recovered, Will was moved to the gentlemen's sleeping quarters near the captain's cabin. Mrs Mott wouldn't hear of him returning to steerage. She secured a first-class ticket for him for the rest of his passage to Melbourne. A young man had died of measles a few days earlier and Will was given his berth and even some of his clothes after they had been boiled.

Will could hardly believe how quickly his fortunes had changed. During the day, he was even allowed to attend school with the children of first-class passengers.

The parents thought it unbecoming that a boy of low breeding should mingle with their offspring and Will was forced to sit a little away from them. For all that, he proved to be a quick learner and by the end of the month, the schoolmaster helped him to pen a letter home.

The Lady Mary
October 29, 1851

My dear Mama,

No ~~dout~~ doubt you will be surprised to see a letter from me. I am well and hope you are too. Has Margret taken over my job with the chestnuts?

It is a fine life here in first-class where I have found myself. The ladies sit on the deck and sketch or sew. The gentlemen smoke their pipes and catch birds and fish.

We are given more food in one day than you would eat in a week.

It is served on very fine china and is most ~~delisus~~ delicious. Currant pudding is my ~~favret~~ favourite.

The ~~emagrents~~ emigrants below deck do not fare so well. They have a diet of soup and dried mutton and oatmeal if they're lucky. Many a poor family has lost children on this voyage. They die of every disease there is going and are tipped into the ocean with great haste. I am thankful I have been rescued from that fearful place called steerage.

I am in the care of Mrs Mott who shows me every kindness. Her husband has taken up a large ~~parsel~~ parcel of land near Ballarat and she is to join him there. It is close by the gold diggings which you may have heard about.

Your loving son,

William

CHAPTER 6

The Theft

"Try this on, William."

Will put down the book he was studying. Mrs Mott stood in the doorway of his cabin smiling warmly. In her hands was a newly sewn jacket. "This should suit you well," she said, with a pleased look.

Another month had passed, and thanks to his regular meals Will was growing out of his clothes at a great rate. He took the jacket with thanks. Mrs Mott treated him like a son, and he was forever grateful to her. The other cabin passengers barely spoke to him though.

Once, Lady Hampton walked out with her nose in the air when he entered the saloon cabin for a glass of water. He heard her tell Mrs Mott loudly so he was sure to hear, "You can't trust the lower classes, Harriet. They'll turn on you in the end."

Will wore his new jacket to the church service that morning. Church was usually held on deck with all classes mingling together. This was one of the rare times when Will would come face-to-face with Mad Dog McGee.

"You're getting above your station," he once said to Will when they passed. But apart from a few sly looks, Mad Dog kept his distance. Will, however, began to feel uneasy and suspected he was hatching a plan.

Today there was a large crowd in attendance—it was expected to be the last Sunday service of the voyage. If the winds were favourable, the *Lady Mary* would reach Port Phillip in a day or so. There was a buzz of excitement on the ship.

As Will opened his prayer book, he felt a nudge in his ribs. He turned to see Mad Dog saunter past, looking pleased with himself. He was up to something, for sure.

A moment later, just as the captain was about to read a prayer, there was a stir among the crowd. Mrs Mott seemed to be in a great state. "My purse," she cried. "It's gone."

The first-class passengers gasped in shock.

Will looked across at Mad Dog, who gave him a sly wink.

The captain took charge immediately. "Steerage passengers remain here," he ordered. "Cabin passengers may retire to the saloon."

Will was about to join the cabin passengers, but the captain stood in his way.

"Not you," he said darkly. "You're as good as steerage."

Mrs Mott's warm brown eyes settled on Will. "William is no thief," she said in her quiet way.

The captain shook his head. "With all respect, Mrs Mott, the lower classes is all the same. They was born to it."

Will puffed his cheeks out with embarrassment and stayed where he was.

He was just about to voice his suspicions but the captain shouted, "Silence!"

The ship's constables were called upon to search pockets and bags. Mad Dog, who had been appointed a constable because of his imposing size, made a great show of searching every passenger. When he reached Will, his face held a sickly smirk. "Turn out your pockets, Will Hawker."

Will froze. They were the very same words Mad Dog had used when he'd bailed Will up on the Liverpool docks.

At that moment, Will realised the awful truth. He had been set up. His hand flew to his jacket pocket. The purse was there all right. He could feel the bulk of it. He felt his cheeks flame red. Everyone was looking at him. He was trapped.

CHAPTER 7

Melbourne, Australia, December 1851

It was the rats that woke him. They made busy scrabbling noises at the end of his bunk. Will didn't move. He had spent the night scratching at lice and fleas and bed-bugs. His bunk was drenched from the seawater that had poured through the hatchway during last night's storm. What was one more discomfort?

In his mind, he turned over the events of yesterday. The shame of being branded a thief. The disappointment etched on Mrs Mott's face. Her blundering attempts to rescue him.

"I remember now," she had said, her voice quavering. "I... I gave the purse to Will. I asked him to look after it."

The captain didn't believe a word but he could not say so in public. Instead, he threw Will back into steerage for the rest of the passage. If it weren't for Mrs Mott's protests, he would have finished the journey in chains.

In some strange way, Will was relieved to be below decks. He could not bear to face Mrs Mott and little Charlotte again.

The bunkroom echoed with the clamour of rattling coughs. A young boy gave a low, rasping moan. From the bunk below came hoarse whispers. Will heard the mention of gold and the new diggings at Ballarat. He carefully turned his head to listen in.

"We'll be rich as lords," said a man's voice.

Will had heard similar talk among the cabin passengers and even the ship's crew. Everyone was fired up at the thought of striking it rich in the colony.

He recognised Mad Dog's throaty chuckle. "There's easy pickings on the goldfields," he said. "An' you don't have to dig for it."

Will wondered what he meant. Knowing Mad Dog, it would be something outside the law.

A few hours later, the cry went up: "Land ahoy!"

Everyone, including Will, was allowed to gather on deck as the ship sailed through Port Phillip Heads. Will leaned over the ship's rail and gazed at the city of Melbourne.

Melbourne

December 2, 1851

Dear Mama,

I have at last arrived in the colony after 94 days at sea. Melbourne is a proper city though many streets are made of dirt. It is warm and the ~~moskitoes~~ mosquitoes are keen as death and feast upon you night and day.

Yesterday I chanced upon a ~~kangeroo~~ kangaroo. They are quite tame and lie about on grassy plots. I have also seen native people about their campfires.

Most are shy and keep to themselves.

Others seem eager to learn and will ask, "What's that fella?" when they want to know the name of something.

I am staying in Canvas Town—a sort of tent village on the banks of the Yarra River. We are all equal here, no matter what our station in life. Meals are shared and help is freely given. (A kindly parson is assisting me with this letter.) Everyone has the same dream—gold. I shall leave for Ballarat as soon as possible and make us all rich.

I hope this letter finds you all well,

Your loving son,

William

CHAPTER 8

Scotch Harry

"Get outta the way!"

Will leapt off the track as a buggy drawn by bullocks almost ran him down. Everyone was in a rush to get to the goldfields. Some had hired dray-carts. Some pushed wheelbarrows laden with their possessions. Others, like Will, carried everything on their backs.

All that day, Will had toiled along. He was almost spent, but figured he had about eighty miles to go. At least his load was light—he carried nothing but a rolled-up blanket, a few clothes, a flask of water and a lump of bread he had scrounged from a baker's shop.

Ahead, something lay on the track. As Will drew closer, he could see that a cart had overturned on the track, spilling its contents. A horse stood grazing nearby.

"Can you give us a hand?" called a red-faced man as Will approached.

In minutes, Will had helped the man right the cart and restore its contents. The man introduced himself as Scotch Harry. He was a barrel-chested Scotsman with gingery whiskers and a ready smile.

"You're welcome to travel along with me, laddie," he told Will, hitching the horse to the cart. "It's safer with two."

"How d'you mean?" asked Will.

"There's plenty of rogues about. Bushrangers, they're called." He paused while he adjusted the horse's harness. "They bail up any vehicles heading south and steal the gold."

That night they made camp by a creek and ate mutton stew, along with some mushrooms they had picked along the way.

The sky was full of stars—brighter than any Will had ever seen. As he wrapped his blanket around himself, his thoughts turned to Mama and his sisters crowded into a damp cellar in the Liverpool slums. Mama had often dreamed of finding a better life. How she and his sisters would enjoy the clear air and open spaces of the colony.

He decided then and there that as soon as he had enough gold, he would pay for their passage out.

"Ballarat is over that hill," Scotch Harry said, a week later. "You can see the smoke from the campfires."

Will sighed with relief. His boots were worn through and his throat was thick with dust. When the settlement came into view, Will's heart began to pound.

His life was about to change; he was sure of it. The township was crowded and there was an air of excitement. Canvas tents and rough humpies filled every space. It seemed that no-one cared how they lived—all thoughts were on gold.

Scotch Harry added William's last few coins to his money and wasted no time in buying a licence and staking a claim on a scrubby hill near a creek.

"I can feel gold all around us, laddie," he said, his blue eyes sparkling. "We'll dig right into the hill and pull out nuggets the size of fists."

Will grinned. He was to be Scotch Harry's sidekick and would share a generous portion of the profits.

"First we must buy ourselves some miner's tools," Scotch Harry said, leading the way towards the canvas-tent shops of the township.

As they reached the main track, two mounted troopers in bright red jackets thundered past at a great pace. Rattling along behind them came an elegant two-wheeled coach with armed troopers on the back. People stood back to let it pass.

"That's the gold escort coach heading for Melbourne," Scotch Harry said in hushed tones. "There's a safe full of gold bolted to the floor inside the carriage."

"The bushrangers wouldn't stand a chance against that lot," said Will, spitting out a mouthful of grit.

Scotch Harry gave him an amused look. "Don't underestimate the power of gold, laddie."

They purchased picks, shovels and pans from a busy shopkeeper and carted everything back to their claim, which they had named Nugget Hill.

The idea was to fill the pan with soil and run creek water across it. The water would carry away the mud, and the heavier gold and pebbles would settle on the bottom of the pan.

The last rays of light beamed through the ironbark bush as they set to work.

"You're a miner now," said Scotch Harry, tossing Will a shovel. "Let's find gold, laddie, and get rich. Then we can get ourselves a farm and a home for your mam and sisters."

CHAPTER 9

Digging for Gold

Will's muscles ached. He stretched his back and gazed at the scene around him. It was a wasteland. Bushes and trees had been ripped from the earth to feed campfires and make way for shovels. Hillocks of spent earth lay scattered about like a vast cemetery with freshly made graves. Down by the creek, scores of miners bent over cradles or pans of swirling mud.

Will kicked a rock into the latest sinkhole he had dug. Like all the others, it produced exactly ... nothing.

It had been almost two months since Scotch Harry staked his claim.

Now everything had been sold to keep the claim going—Nelly the horse, the dray-cart, even Scotch Harry's oilskin coat. But day after day of backbreaking work had turned up nothing—not even an ounce of gold dust.

If they didn't find gold soon, they would lose the claim. Every month, troopers from the Native Police Corps arrived to demand the licence fee.

Will was about to carry another load of soil to the creek when he heard a strange sound, almost like choking. It was coming from the deep sinkhole where Scotch Harry had been working all morning. Will knelt down. "Is everything all right?"

"Bring me a lantern, lad!" said Scotch Harry, whose voice had become a squeak. "And mind you don't run."

With the lantern delivered, Will waited. A few moments later, Scotch Harry emerged with something wrapped in his shirt. His eyes held a strange gleam.

"What is it?" breathed Will.

"Come close and I'll tell ye," Scotch Harry whispered excitedly. "Try to act natural."

Scotch Harry's eyes darted about as he grabbed Will's wrist. "We're rich, laddie," he hissed. "This here nugget is the size of an egg."

Will's breath caught in his throat. At last! He thought immediately of Mama and his sisters. Now they would be able to join him in the colony. All would be well.

In hushed tones, the two made a plan. Will would carry the nugget in his jacket pocket and make his way to the Gold Office to deposit it. He would take a shortcut through the gully to avoid the miners along the creek. Scotch Harry would continue to work the sinkhole as if it was an ordinary day.

Will set off immediately, his heart hammering like a bailiff's fist.

Although it was mid-autumn, the air was hot and still. Sweat trickled down his face like a crawling insect. He kept his head down but his eyes shunted from one tree to the next. Spiked leaves prodded his legs and dry grasses whispered against his boots.

He had almost reached the main road when it happened. A low whinny from a horse almost made him jump out of his skin.

Behind a clump of wattle sat a rider, as still as a stone. In his lap lay a double-barrel rifle. It was aimed at Will's chest.

"Don't move," said the rider quietly.

The man had a dark bushy beard and black boots that came over his knees. His rope belt held a pistol.

His dark eyes darted from Will to the road. That was when Will noticed two riders on the other side, half-hidden by trees.

Bushrangers! Will's hand flew to his pocket where the nugget lay wrapped in a handkerchief. He rammed it down with his fist.

In the distance came the thud of hooves and the clatter of carriage wheels.

"Start moving," said the rider to Will, motioning with his rifle. "Walk into the road."

"Wait a minute—" Will began.

"Do it!"

A spiral of dust rose above the trees. The carriage was almost upon them.

Reluctantly Will set foot on the road just as the carriage bucked and swayed around the corner.

"Whoa!" cried the coach's driver, pulling hard on the reins.

The bushrangers made their move. Firing shots into the air, they galloped alongside the carriage. One of them—a gangly youth with hollow cheeks—grabbed the lead horse and brought it to a halt.

"Bail up!" cried Bushy Beard.

The carriage door was yanked open and four frozen-faced passengers stepped out.

"Hand over everything you have."

Will saw his chance. A mullock heap on the side of the road was high enough to give him some cover. He crept towards it.

"Hey you!"

A spasm of terror jolted through him as if he had been shot. He turned slowly, hoping his face showed no emotion.

The hollow-cheeked bushranger was looking hard at him, licking his lips. He was young—no more than fourteen.

He waved a pistol towards Will's face but his voice was calm and soft. "Are you from around here?"

"Yeh."

"I'm real hungry," said the youth. "Have you got any food?"

Will felt a flash of relief. "No. I've got nothing."

Hollow Cheeks pointed his pistol at Will's jacket. "What's in your pocket?"

Will's heart turned cold. "Nothing."

"What sort of nothing?"

"A handkerchief. That's all." The words rushed out too quickly.

The boy's eyes glinted. "Show me."

Will hesitated. Hollow Cheeks raised the pistol. "If it's a gun or a knife, I'll shoot ya."

Will thought about making a run for it but he knew the pistol was loaded. With a heavy heart, he pulled out the handkerchief and unwrapped it. The nugget lay heavy in his hand.

Hollow Cheeks snatched the nugget and let out a whoop. "Is that thing real?"

Without waiting for an answer, he dismounted from his horse and barrelled over to the group by the carriage.

Will turned for the scrub. The bushrangers could shoot him for all he cared. Nothing mattered now.

CHAPTER 10

A New Start

Will huddled under the bridge. It was mid-winter and a soft drizzle fell. The roads of Ballarat had turned to muck long ago. His clothes, what was left of them, were thick with mud. He hadn't eaten for days and his stomach was cramped with hunger. He couldn't believe he could ever be so cold and hungry.

He thought of Scotch Harry who lost his gold claim when the licence ran out. He had taken up work as a fencer. Will heard he had done some work on the biggest sheep station in the district—owned by the Motts.

Harriet Mott! How Will wished he could visit her and little Charlotte. Mrs Mott had always been so kind to him. But now she believed he was a thief. She would never welcome him in her house. The thought was almost too much to bear.

Will rubbed his thin hands, shivering in the frosty air. He needed to walk to keep warm. The mud curled around his bare feet as he followed the track to the Chinese market gardens. Rows of green vegetables met his eye. If it weren't for the Chinese gardeners, the miners would have nothing to eat but meat and damper. Careful not to be seen, Will grabbed a handful of cabbage leaves and stuffed them in his mouth.

His belly began to heave and he thought he would be sick. He crept under an ironbark tree and lay there breathing heavily. He closed his eyes and his thoughts turned to Mama and his sisters. How he missed them all and longed to see them again.

It was the thud of horse hooves that brought Will back to his senses. He heard the creak of a saddle and the slow clump of boots. Something prodded him in the back.

"Get up."

Will turned slowly, his ribs aching. There was no way he could stand up. He was too weak. Will looked up warily. The man was huge, built like a bull. There was something familiar about him, but Will was too sick to care.

Suddenly the world seemed to be swaying. He was being lifted, hoisted over the horse saddle like a sack of flour. Then his mind fell into…

Nothing.

The next thing Will felt was warmth. Lovely warmth all the way through to his bones. He smiled, enjoying this dream.

He became aware of something heavy lying over him—a coat perhaps. Then he smelt a fire and meat cooking.

"Take this, Will Hawker."

He lifted his face and gazed into the shark-grey eyes of Mad Dog McGee. His tattooed hand held a mug of tea.

"Drink it. You need it."

Will blinked for a moment. A thousand questions flooded his mind. Then his thin hand closed around the mug. The steam filled his nostrils. He drank greedily.

With his belly full of tea and then stew, and the coat heavy around his shoulders, Will's mind began to clear. His eyes flickered across to Mad Dog, who was poking the fire with a stick.

He felt amazed and confused all at once. Mad Dog was his enemy. Why had he helped him?

Mad Dog seemed to read his thoughts. "We're even, Will Hawker," he said. "I paid you back good and proper on the *Lady Mary*."

"But—"

"This is a new colony. A new start," Mad Dog said. "We Liverpool lads have to stick together."

He tossed a blanket at Will. "Get some sleep. You've got a big day tomorrow."

Will drifted into sleep again, wondering what he meant.

CHAPTER 11

The Gold Office

"All you have to do is wait here and hold my horse," Mad Dog was saying. He dragged a canvas sack from his saddlebag. "We'll be counting gold by sundown."

Will's mind reeled. They were standing across the road from the crudely built office where miners paid for their licences and cashed in their gold. McGee was planning to hold the place up and steal everything he could carry.

Will's eyes scanned the street. It was crowded with people, some entering and leaving the Gold Office door. A small boy came up to Will and patted the chestnut mare he was holding. Mad Dog had procured two mares only that morning. Will didn't ask where they came from, but he now understood their purpose. He and Mad Dog would both need fast horses to make their getaway into the nearby hills.

Mad Dog turned to face Will. "Are you ready?"

Will backed away, almost falling into the horse trough. "No!" He couldn't do it. He would be no worse than a bushranger—an outlaw hunted down by trackers and troopers.

Mad Dog's grey eyes fixed on Will. "I'll give you a fair share. I swear it." He lowered his voice to a fierce whisper. "You'll have enough to pay the fare for your mama and sisters on a good ship."

Will swallowed hard. The thought of his family almost made him cry. What he would give to see them again! "Will anyone get shot?" he asked, eyeing the pistol in Mad Dog's belt.

"Not a chance," Mad Dog said, crisply. His eyes strayed to the red-coated trooper leaning casually against a water cart.

"What if someone escapes?" Will whispered.

"They won't. I'll lock the door." Mad Dog looked squarely at him. "Trust me, Hawker. I've done this before."

All of a sudden, Will knew what he had to do. He found himself nodding. "All right," he said. "I'm ready."

"Good lad." Mad Dog drew his horse forward.

"Here—take the reins. When I run out of the Gold Office, jump onto your horse." He patted Will's back in a friendly way. "Get ready to ride hard."

Will's eyes followed Mad Dog as he crossed the road and disappeared through the Gold Office door. A wave of sickness flooded him. He could hardly believe what was he was doing.

At that moment, the mare's soft muzzle brushed his cheek and he gave a start. His eyes darted to the trooper leaning against the water cart. He had been joined by others … four, no … five more troopers. The town was crawling with them!

"Hello William!"

Will spun around. Who could be calling him? There was only one person in all of Ballarat who would call him by his full name … and there she was, crossing the road towards him. Mrs Mott!

He couldn't speak. His mouth was as dry as cotton.

“So you’ve made it to Ballarat,” Mrs Mott said, warmly. “I’m very pleased, William. This is a fine country with many opportunities for a young man.”

Will nodded, unable to speak. His eyes darted towards the Gold Office. Any minute now, Mad Dog would burst out of it.

Mrs Mott leaned towards Will and her deep brown eyes gazed into his. “I want you to know something, William,” she said in a serious tone. “I’ve become quite convinced that it was not you who took my purse.” She reached out her gloved hand and squeezed his arm. “You are not a thief. I know it.”

As nervous as he was, Will managed a smile.

“How have you been?” asked Mrs Mott. “You look very thin and drawn.”

At that moment, the door to the Gold Office burst open.

CHAPTER 12

Bound for the Colony

Will acted swiftly. "Get down and stay there!" he said to Mrs Mott, pulling her behind the horse trough. He let out a blood-curdling cry and smacked the horses' rumps, sending them bolting wide-eyed into the middle of the road.

Then, he ran.

The troopers were laughing at someone's joke, but they soon stopped when Will came crashing towards them. He had counted on one trooper, but six would make the task much easier.

He poured out enough words to cause an instant response. The troopers took up their firearms and charged towards Mad Dog, who now stood in the roadway with a dazed look. His mouth was still gaping open when they arrested him.

"I'll get you for this, Will Hawker!" he cried, as they led him away. But his words were hollow.

"Dear William!" Mrs Mott beamed from under her broad-brimmed hat. "How brave you were. Yet again, you have saved the day."

Will returned her smile. All would be well now. He knew it.

Ballarat
March 8, 1852

Dearest Mama,

Your dearly awaited letter arrived at last and it gives me great joy to know that you and my sisters are all well. It seems such a long time since I left home and much has happened. I now find myself on a sheep station outside Ballarat. It is owned by Mr Mott, who wants me to help him farm sheep.

Enclosed, you will find tickets for first-class fares to Melbourne. Enough for all of you. One day, I will tell you the story of how I came by this wealth. For now, let me just say that it came as a reward for the capture of a bushranger.

I find the life here most agreeable and I'm sure you will too.

Your loving son,

William